Bears

Michael and Jane Pelusey

 **Marshall Cavendish**
Benchmark
New York

This edition first published in 2009 in the United States of America by Marshall Cavendish Benchmark.

Marshall Cavendish Benchmark
99 White Plains Road
Tarrytown, NY 10591
www.marshallcavendish.us

All Internet sites were available and accurate when sent to press.

First published in 2008 by
MACMILLAN EDUCATION AUSTRALIA PTY LTD
15–19 Claremont Street, South Yarra 3141

Visit our Web site at www.macmillan.com.au or go directly to www.macmillanlibrary.com.au

Associated companies and representatives throughout the world.

Library of Congress Cataloging-in-Publication Data

Pelusey, Michael.
  Bears / by Michael and Jane Pelusey.
  p. cm. — (Zoo animals)
  Includes index.
  ISBN 978-0-7614-3147-3
  1. Bears—Juvenile literature. 2. Zoo animals—Juvenile literature. I.
  Pelusey, Jane. II. Title.
  SF408.6.B43P45 2008
  636.978—dc22
                                                              2008001647

Edited by Margaret Maher
Text and cover design by Christine Deering
Page layout by Christine Deering
Illustrations by Gaston Vanzet

Printed in the United States

Acknowledgments
Michael and Jane Pelusey would like to thank Sea World, Perth Zoo, Melbourne Zoo, Werribee Wildlife Zoo, and Taronga Zoo for their assistance with this project.

Cover photograph: Male and female brown bear in zoo enclosure, courtesy of Pelusey Photography.

All photographs © Pelusey Photography except for © Jmphoto/Dreamstime.com, 28; Taronga Zoo, 7 (top left); Save the Bears, 6, 20, 30; Sea World, 7 (top right), 11, 13, 14, 17, 19 (top and bottom), 22, 26, 27; © Condor 36/Shutterstock, 29; kristian sekulic /Shutterstock, 18; Taronga Zoo, 7 (top left).

1 3 5 6 4 2

Contents

Glossary words

When a word is printed in **bold**, you can look up its meaning in the Glossary on page 31.

Zoos

Zoos are places where animals that are usually **wild** are kept in **enclosures**. Some zoos have a lot of space for animals to move about. They are often called wildlife zoos.

A wildlife zoo has a lot of space for large animals to roam.

Zoo Animals

Zoos keep all kinds of animals. People go to zoos to learn about animals. Some animals may become **extinct** if left to live in the wild.

People watch a bear in an enclosure.

5

Bears

Bears are powerful animals with big claws. There are different kinds of bears. The polar bear is white. The giant panda is black and white.

The sun bear is black with a yellow stripe on its chest.

The Kodiak bear is the biggest bear in the world.
It is a type of brown bear. The sun bear is
the smallest bear.

Polar bears are almost as
large as Kodiak bears.

Brown bears are very large.

The giant panda is one of the
smaller kinds of bear in the world.

The sun bear is the
smallest of all the bears.

In the Wild

In the wild, bears live mainly in the forests of Asia, North America, and Europe. Most bears eat fruit, berries, and insects, and hunt small animals.

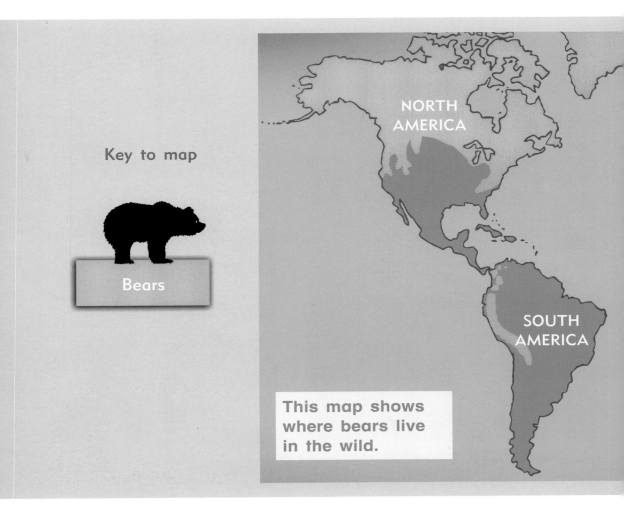

Key to map

Bears

NORTH AMERICA

SOUTH AMERICA

This map shows where bears live in the wild.

Polar bears live in the northern part of the world.
They live in the cold **Arctic** region.

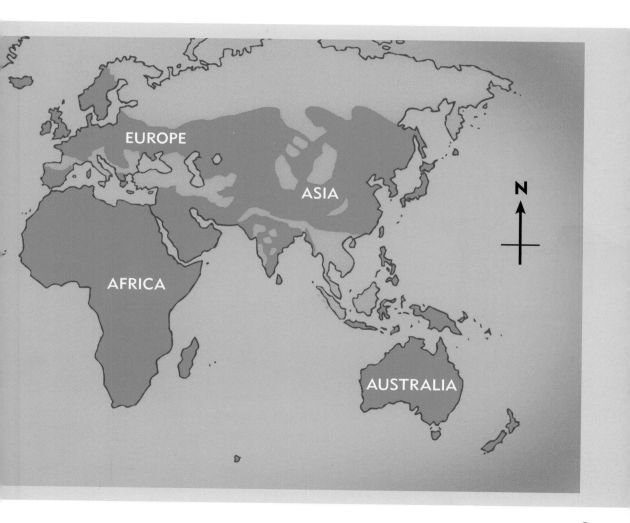

Threats to Survival

The biggest threat to survival for most bears is forest clearing for timber and farming.

When a forest is cleared for farming, there are fewer places for bears to live.

Polar bears are threatened because warm seas
are melting the **ice sheets** where they hunt seals.

A polar bear hunts in the snow and on ice sheets.

Zoo Homes

In zoos, bears live in enclosures. These enclosures are often built so they are like the bears' home in the wild.

tree for shade

night enclosure

toys to play with

logs to climb on

rocks to climb and lie on

An enclosure usually has features that make it like the bears' natural home.

Polar bears need plenty of water to keep cool in hot weather.

sails for shade

trees for shade

rocks to climb on

toys to play with

deep pool of water

The polar bear enclosure has a deep pool of water for the bears to swim in.

Zoo Food

Bears need to eat different types of food to stay healthy.

A sun bear's zoo food
fruit
vegetables
Give the sun bear a bone once a week.

A polar bear's zoo food
fish
vegetables
bones
meat
Make sure some of the polar bear's meals are frozen.

A brown bear's zoo food
fish
meat
fruit
vegetables

A polar bear uses its sharp claws and teeth to eat a frozen watermelon.

Feeding

Bears use their claws to dig for roots and to pull food apart. They have strong jaws and big teeth to crunch meat and bones.

A brown bear uses its strong jaws to bite through a hard bone.

Zoo Health

Zookeepers clean the enclosures every day to make sure the bears stay healthy. They check that the bears are eating well and are active.

A zookeeper throws food to the brown bears and checks their health.

Large bears can be dangerous even when they are sick. They need to be **tranquilized** before a **veterinarian** can treat them.

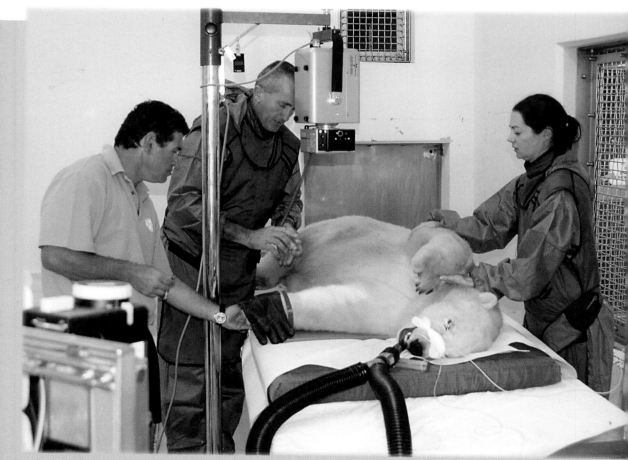

A polar bear is tranquilized while it has an X-ray.

Baby Bears

A mother bear has one or two **cubs** at a time. It takes from three to eight months for a baby bear to grow inside its mother.

A mother bear is followed by her two cubs.

Female polar bears care for their cubs for two to three years.

A female polar bear cares for her cub.

This polar bear has two cubs.

How Zoos Are Saving Bears

Many kinds of bear are **endangered**. There are few sun bears left in the wild. Zoos are breeding sun bears to increase their numbers.

Endangered sun bears are bred at zoos.

Zoos also work with other groups. The Free The Bears Fund rescues bears that have been kept by people and badly treated. The bears are released into protected wild areas or kept in some zoos.

This sun bear was badly treated, but now lives in a zoo.

Zoos work together by sharing bears. If one zoo has too many bears, they send some to other zoos. Giant pandas from China are sometimes lent to zoos in other countries.

A polar bear moves from an Australian zoo to an American zoo.

Sun bears need enclosures that are similar to their natural homes. Visitors donate money to zoos to make new enclosures.

This sign is asking people to donate money for new bear enclosures.

Meet Adrian, a Bear Keeper

Adrian has worked with bears for five years.

Question   How did you become a zookeeper?

Answer   I studied to be a zookeeper. Then I did volunteer work with the zoo until a job came up.

Question   How long have you been a keeper?

Answer   I have been a keeper for twelve years.

Adrian throws meat to the male bear.

Question   What animals have you worked with?

Answer   I have worked with most animals in the zoo.

Question   What do you like about your job?

Answer   I like working with animals, because every day is different.

A Day in the Life of a Zookeeper

Zookeepers have jobs to do each day. Some keepers work with bears. Polar bears are looked after by a team of keepers.

8:00 a.m.

Clean the bears' day enclosure while the bears are still in their night enclosures.

9:00 a.m.

Feed the bears before they go out into the day enclosure.

12:30 p.m.

Give the bears a toy to play with.

3:00 p.m.

Turn on the cooling mist to help the bears cool off in the heat of the day.

Zoos Around the World

There are zoos all around the world.
The Smithsonian National Zoo is in Washington, D.C.
This zoo keeps three very rare giant pandas.

Tai Shan is a baby giant panda that was born at the Smithsonian National Zoo.

The giant panda enclosure at the Smithsonian has rocky places and trees to climb. The pandas keep cool in the streams and waterfall on hot days.

This giant panda relaxes in its enclosure at the Smithsonian.

The Importance of Zoos

Zoos do very important work. They:

- help people learn about animals
- save endangered animals and animals that are treated badly

Zoos play an important role in saving endangered sun bears.

Glossary

Arctic   the area around the North Pole

breed   keep animals so that they can produce babies

cubs   baby bears

enclosures   the fenced areas where animals are kept in zoos

endangered   at a high risk of becoming extinct

extinct   no longer living on Earth

ice sheets   large areas of ice that cover the sea around the North Pole

tranquilized   given a drug that makes the animal unconscious

veterinarian   a doctor who treats animals

wild   living in its natural environment and not taken care of by humans

Index